CW00797589

Contents

Introduction
What has happened to Sundays?

Much Sunday worship is struggling

The big picture is that our society is secular. The God of the Bible is dismissed as irrelevant—probably not even there. It is not surprising therefore that church attendance has halved in the last forty years. Though the population of the UK has jumped from around 56 million in 1980 to 67 million now—an increase of approximately 20%—yet church attendance has dropped drastically. These facts sadden the heart of any Christian who cares about the glory of Jesus and the salvation of our fellow men and women.

JUNE						**?**
M	T	W	T	F	S	
	1	2	3	4	5	
6	7	8	9	10	11	12
13	14	15	16	17	18	19
20	21	22	23	24	25	26
27	28	29	30			

But in the more recent time frame, churches are still handling gathering again as we slowly emerge from the Covid pandemic. From March 2020, with intermissions, churches and other places where people assemble were closed for the public good. Most churches went online. This was tough. But the process of re-gathering congregations 'in church' is proving more difficult than we had been led to expect. We had hoped that Christians would be keen to meet up again once restrictions were lifted. There are so many enjoyable features of Sunday church that are simply not possible online. We can't sing together to the Lord and to each other (Colossians 3:16). We can't take the Lord's Supper together or encourage one another in the same way (1 Thessalonians 5:11). Yet the return to church has been slow. Many have been lost from church. Many simply want to continue to do church from home because it feels safer and it is more convenient. So this too contributes to why Sunday worship is in difficulties.

Yet at the same time as the church is struggling like this, there has been an undermining of the Sabbath commandment in much Christian teaching. Though the Fourth of the Ten Words of the Decalogue has always been seen as foundational to weekly worship, it is now often disputed or discounted theologically. The day of rest and worship has been relegated to an option. Many pastors and preachers have adopted a 'nine out of ten' view of the Ten Commandments. Surely with Sunday church attendance dwindling, we need to consider this matter?

This booklet will argue for a 'ten out of ten' view and that the Sabbath command—yes, it has changed somewhat with the coming of the new covenant in Christ—is still an imperative for Christians.

1 The attack on the day of rest

The idea that Sunday worship, Sunday church attendance, is part of Christian obedience is increasingly out of fashion and spoken of in equivocal terms or even opposed by many in positions of evangelical leadership today. A couple of New Testament references are frequently used to support this rejection of the idea of the Sabbath.

For example, Romans 14:5 says, 'One man considers one day more sacred than another; another man considers every day alike. Each one should be fully convinced in his own mind.' Here Paul is considering Christian freedom of conscience in terms of 'the weak' and 'the strong'.

SUNDAY = MONDAY = TUESDAY = WEDNESDAY = THURSDAY = FRIDAY = SATURDAY

The *ESV Study Bible* (which is great in many ways) carries this comment: *'The weak thought some days were more important than others. Given the Jewish background here that day supremely in view is certainly the Sabbath. The strong think every day is the same. Both views are permissible. Each person must follow his own conscience. What is remarkable is that the Sabbath is no longer a binding commitment for Paul but a matter of one's personal conviction. Unlike the other 9 commandments in Exodus 20:1–17 the Sabbath command seems to be part of the ceremonial laws of the Mosaic Covenant which are no longer binding. However, it is still wise to take regular times of rest and regular times of worship are commanded for Christians.'*

Many modern evangelicals would concur with that statement. They would say that actually Sunday isn't special. The Decalogue is divided. Some commands still hold. At least one doesn't. We can practically strike out the Fourth Commandment. There is no longer any kind of obligation before God to take rest and engage in his worship with his people on a set day of the week. Following the *ESV Study Bible*, it is a matter of wisdom as to whether you take a day off and go to church on Sunday—like perhaps skipping a meal or a workout at the gym. 'Do I really need this?' we can ask.

Pragmatism

It leads to Christians becoming increasingly loose and pragmatic about Sundays and what they do. 'We'll fit in church somewhere, perhaps before we go out to the beach or late afternoon on way back from the supermarket'; because Sunday isn't special.

And, of course, adopting such an outlook concerning the Ten Commandments has other implications. If one has become optional—the Sabbath—what are we to

'We'll fit in church somewhere'

make of the rest of them? Perhaps they are somewhat optional too? Perhaps, for example, it is just a matter of wisdom as to whether or not I tell a lie?

The question must be, 'Is the *ESV* footnote correct?'[1] Is this the right interpretation of Romans 14:5 and similar verses like Colossians 2:16–17? Is it right to conclude from these verses that one of the Ten Commandments 'is no longer binding'? Or have we rushed to embrace something that appeals to us as 21st century Western consumers as an easier option? In the rest of this booklet, I will explain why I think this explanation has got it wrong.

Prima facie case

Though many well-known and gifted contemporary theologians adopt this striking out of the Fourth Commandment, we need to think for ourselves.

But before we get into the argument, here are two initial Biblical reasons regarding why we should be sceptical of this position. It is very unlikely to be true because...

First, there is no explicit rescinding of the Sabbath commandment in the New Testament. Some say that the Sabbath commandment is nowhere directly promulgated in the New Testament and that is good enough for them to dismiss it—we will come back to that. But my response is that nowhere does the New Testament explicitly reject the idea of a weekly day of rest and worship as being God's will for us. It may dismiss the Jewish Sabbath day of the Old Covenant. But there is nowhere which says a day for God has no place in the New Covenant.

Though this is an argument from silence it carries weight, because other laws from the Old Testament are specifically cancelled in the New Testament. For example...

---

1. I am picking on the *ESV Study Bible* footnote simply to focus the discussion, but I could have used other examples.

- The food laws of the Old Testament are abolished. After recording the Lord Jesus saying, 'nothing that enters a man from the outside can make him "unclean"', Mark tells us plainly in his Gospel, 'In saying this, Jesus declared all foods "clean"' (Mark 7:18, 19).

Food ABOLISHED laws

Jesus declared all foods 'clean'

- The racial laws of the Old Testament are cancelled. After his vision on the rooftop, Peter declares to the Gentile centurion Cornelius and his friends, 'God has shown me that I should not call any man impure or unclean' (Acts 10:28).

Racial CANCELLED laws

'God has shown me that I should not call any man impure or unclean'

- The sacrificial laws of the Old Testament are rescinded. The whole New Testament epistle to the Hebrews teaches this. The sacrifice of Christ is once for all.

Sacrificial laws RESCINDED

Christ 'has appeared once for all at the end of the ages to put away sin by the sacrifice of himself'

The Ten Commandments

I
Thou shalt have no other gods before me

II
Thou shalt not make unto thee any graven image

III
Thou shalt not take the name of the LORD thy God in vain

IV
Remember the sabbath day to keep it holy

V
Honour thy father and thy mother

VI
Thou shalt not kill

VII
Thou shalt not commit adultery

VIII
Thou shalt not steal

IX
Thou shalt not bear false witness against thy neighbour

X
Thou shalt not covet

But there is no similar indication that a weekly day for God no longer applies. Surely if, for example, Mark makes the cancellation of the Old Testament food laws explicit, if there had been a cancellation of one of the Ten Commandments, it would have been made crystal clear. But it isn't.

Second, notice that the writer of the *ESV Study Bible*'s comments tries to regularise the removal of the Fourth Commandment by re-categorising it as a ceremonial law. No doubt there were some ceremonial aspects of the Jewish Sabbath, however the essence of the Sabbath is not ceremonial but moral. This command declares to those in positions of power that it is a sin before God to make people work seven days a week with no day for rest. In fact, the version of the Ten Commandments recorded in Deuteronomy specifically links the ignoring of the Sabbath command with slavery:

> 'Observe the Sabbath day by keeping it holy …
> Remember that you were slaves in Egypt and the LORD
> your God brought you out of there with a mighty
> hand …' (Deuteronomy 5:12–15).

Apart from anything else, this is a piece of employment law with a moral purpose of loving our fellow human beings by protecting people from abuse. Is such a law likely to be rescinded by the New Covenant?

This is a piece of employment law with a moral purpose

For these reasons alone, we ought to be hesitant about simply accepting the *ESV Study Bible*'s interpretation of how we understand the Sabbath command now.

The Ten Commandments

I
Thou shalt have no other gods before me

II
Thou shalt not make unto thee any graven image

III
Thou shalt not take the name of the LORD thy God in vain

IV
Remember the sabbath day to keep it holy

V
Honour thy father and thy mother

VI
Thou shalt not kill

VII
Thou shalt not commit adultery

VIII
Thou shalt not steal

IX
Thou shalt not bear false witness against thy neighbour

X
Thou shalt not covet

2 The New Testament data

The matter of how to view the Sabbath command in the light of the life, death and resurrection of Christ clearly involves the question of precisely how the Old Testament relates to the New Testament. This is a complicated question (which we will look at) and over which great theologians differ. But we must not miss the wood for the trees. Let's step back for a moment.

Days for strong Christians?

We must first ask a question. Is it true that strong Christians in the New Testament regarded all days the same and no day as special? When Romans 14:5 states 'another man considers every day alike'—was that meant to be taken as an absolute statement? Did it mean that Christians with robust and mature consciences treated every day of the week the same?

SUNDAY = MONDAY = TUESDAY = WEDNESDAY = THURSDAY = FRIDAY = SATURDAY

The answer is 'No.'

The apostle John (a strong Christian, I think we can assume) obviously thought that during the week there was a special day—he calls it 'the Lord's Day' (Revelation 1:10).[2] He clearly saw a certain day as marked out, to be differentiated from other days of the week. He did not consider 'all days alike'.

THE LORD'S DAY

MONDAY TUESDAY WEDNESDAY THURSDAY FRIDAY SATURDAY

Furthermore, we find that the early church gathered on a particular day—the first day of the week (Acts 20:7). That was understood as the general practice. They did not regard Tuesday or Thursday as being as appropriate as Sunday to gather for worship.

And the apostle Paul (a strong Christian) encourages Christians to have their collections to help other churches when they regularly get together—on the first day of the week (1 Corinthians 16:2).

Surely, reflecting on this data, we see that all days were not regarded as the same. We see that the idea of understanding Romans 14:5 in absolute terms, implying that it applies across

---

2   To make out, as some try to, that 'the Lord's Day' here refers to the whole New Covenant period or the last days until Christ's return would make the phrase redundant in the sentence. Also John's use of sevens in his structuring of Revelation indicates that he still frames everything in terms of the Creation week including the Sabbath.

the board, seems to be leading to a quite definite problem. Strong Christians did not think of every day of the week as the same.

Indeed, Paul would be contradicting himself. He clearly did think of the first day of the week as different from other days.

The first day of the week

Logically, the next question we must ask is, 'Who inaugurated the idea of the church gathering on the first day of the week?'

As we dig into the New Testament, we realise that the idea of the first day of the week being special was not something pragmatic or dreamed up by the early Christians as Romans 14:5 would imply if we take the *ESV Study Bible* footnote understanding. Look at the data. We find that this idea of meeting together with the Lord on Sundays is something clearly instigated by God himself.

The first day of the week is the Lord's Day because on that day Jesus rose from the dead—thus declaring that he is Lord of all (Romans 1:4).

The first day of the week is the Lord's Day

And it is surely noteworthy that although Jesus probably was crucified on a Friday, none of the Gospels make that explicit. But by complete contrast all four Gospels spell out repeatedly that Jesus rose on Sunday, the first day of the week.

- 'After the Sabbath, at dawn on the first day of the week, Mary Magdalene and the other Mary went to look at the tomb' (Matthew 28:1).

- 'Very early on the first day of the week, just after sunrise, they were on their way to the tomb and they asked each other, "Who will roll the stone away from the entrance of the tomb?"' (Mark 16:2–3).

- 'On the first day of the week, very early in the morning, the women took the spices they had prepared and went to the tomb' (Luke 24:1).

- 'Early on the first day of the week, while it was still dark, Mary Magdalene went to the tomb and saw that the stone had been removed from the entrance' (John 20:1).

Unlike the day Jesus died, the Gospels leave us in no doubt as to the day Jesus rose from the tomb in the power of an endless life.

The day for church

It was Sunday on which God raised Jesus from the dead and it was also the day on which the risen Lord first met with his disciples.[3] The Gospel of John specifically underlines that it was 'on the evening of that first day of the week' that Jesus came to his disciples as they were in hiding (John 20:19).

And not only was the resurrection on a Sunday with Jesus meeting with his disciples on that day, the Gospels go on to tell us that Jesus met with his disciples in an ongoing way on Sunday. Thomas had not been present when Jesus, alive from the dead, had first appeared to his disciples behind locked doors. But it was just 'a week later', again therefore on the first day of the week, that he met with them again. This time Thomas was present and, of course, Jesus answered his famous doubts (John 20:19,26).[4]

> It was not something they simply thought 'wise'

The idea of church on Sunday was not something which the church initiated or decided upon to suit themselves. It was not something they simply thought 'wise'. It was something God himself started. The risen

---

3 Matthew 28:8–9; Mark 16:9; Luke 24:15,30,31; John 20:19.
4 Thomas becomes a Sunday worshipper, calling Jesus, 'My Lord and my God' (John 20:28).

Lord deliberately went looking for them to meet with them on the first day of the week.

What is the essence of church? It is surely Jesus meeting with his people. And now Jesus is ascended, we do that as he comes to us by his Word and his Spirit. And guess which day of the week the Holy Spirit came? Pentecost was a Sunday (check it out: Leviticus 23:15–16).

So, in the New Testament there was obviously a God-appointed special day—Sunday, one day every seven—which the church observed, the day they met together. The idea that strong Christians treated every day alike doesn't stack up with the evidence.

3 Jews and Gentiles

How then are we to understand Romans 14:5 and Colossians 2:16–17? If they don't teach that there is now no need for a day of rest or a special day for the church to gather, then what do they teach?

Surely the answer is fairly straightforward once we realise the background in both cases. In Romans there is a question about Jew and Gentile believers relating together in the same church. In Colossians there are troubles caused by heretical ideas which have, at least partially, a Jewish origin.

Romans

The historical situation against which Paul writes his great gospel epistle to the churches in Rome is significant.

In AD 49 the emperor Claudius had banned all Jews from Rome. This may well have come about due to breaches of the peace within the Jewish community when the gospel first came to the city. Some Jews reacted badly to the idea that Jesus is their Messiah. The disturbances were so violent, it would appear, that the emperor banished all Jews—whether they were Christians or not.[5] So, the churches in Rome at that point became exclusively Gentile for a time. The congregations and leaders were

OUT OF ROME!
By order of the Emperor Claudius

---

5   The book of Acts mentions this as it describes how Paul first met Priscilla and Aquila when he was staying in Corinth, 'There he met a Jew named Aquila, a native of Pontus, who had recently come from Italy with his wife Priscilla, because Claudius had ordered all the Jews to leave Rome' (Acts 18:2).

Gentile, because they were the only Christians left. Hence for some years before Paul wrote, the Roman churches had not been used to having Jewish folk among them. This meant that the culture of the churches changed somewhat. They lost sensitivity with regard to welcoming and including people from a different background to their own.

However, with the accession of Nero in AD 54, the Jews had begun gradually to return. But because church had changed so much the Jewish Christians felt like outsiders. That led to tensions between the two groups. The unity of the churches was threatened. Hence, part of Paul's motivation in writing the epistle is to try to show how Jewish and Gentile Christians must get along together. The gospel is for all. Especially in the early chapters, we find the recurring phrase, 'first for the Jew, then for the Gentile' (Romans 1:16, etc.). Both need Christ. He is the Saviour of all who believe, whatever their background (Romans 4:11–12). And when we come to chapters 14 and 15, Paul is instructing the church concerning what it means practically to accept one another and handle different sensitivities related to conscience and cultural backgrounds.

The gospel is for all

What is primarily in view in Romans 14:5, given this context, is the Old Testament Jewish calendar of Saturday Sabbaths and feasts. That's all gone. Those are things no longer obligatory now Christ has come. When Paul in Romans 14:5 speaks of considering 'every day alike' he is not speaking absolutely, but in the context of the Jewish calendar. But if a Jewish Christian personally wants to continue to keep the Jewish Sabbath or a Jewish feast (as well as, presumably, being with his church on Sunday)—that is completely within their liberty—indeed Paul himself seems to do this sometimes (Acts 20:16). Jewish and Gentile Christians should not condemn one another, but accept each other over such matters. That is the heart of what Paul is saying.

15

But though the Jewish calendar is finished—fulfilled in Christ—to infer from that that there are now no special days absolutely is to infer something that simply does not follow from what Paul is explaining and leads, as we have seen, to contradiction. The Jewish Sabbath having gone is one thing—but to conclude from that that the whole Sabbath principle has gone is quite another.

Colossians

If what Paul writes in Romans concerning the Sabbath is misunderstood to promote the idea of a complete abandonment of the idea of a weekly day, special to God, then the reference in Colossians addresses the opposite error. This is that Christians must keep the Jewish calendar.

The letter to the Colossians was written by Paul primarily to combat a certain type of false teaching. We can label this the 'Not only … but also…' heresy. This erroneous idea was that although we must accept Jesus as our Saviour, he does not save us completely. More is needed in order to acquire 'fullness' or full fellowship with God. Other mediators were required.[6] Various ceremonies and aesthetic practices were said to be needed.[7] Not only personal trust in Jesus, but also other things are necessary. And if you were not following these religious extras, you were second-rate or even to be discounted.

Christ alone

These things were not to be seen as optional but obligatory for the true Christian. But, of course, once we start insisting on things like that, our faith is subtly shifted away from Christ to these other things—to the things we do and think we have power to control. It is no longer Christ alone, but other mediators and our own devotion, expressed in various ways, that saves us.

---

6 Colossians 2:18.
7 Colossians 2:16,21–23.

Among these 'religious extras' that the false teaching in Colosse insisted on, were various aspects of Old Testament Jewish practices. It is in opposing this Jewish-flavoured heresy that Paul writes:

> 'Therefore do not let anyone judge you by what you eat or drink, or with regard to a religious festival, a New Moon celebration or a Sabbath day. These are a shadow of the things that were to come; the reality, however, is found in Christ' (Colossians 2:16–17).

Once more it is clear that what Paul has in mind here is that the Old Testament Jewish calendar is finished. A full relationship with God is not dependent on such observances but only on Christ and faith in him. But again, to reason from this that there is a total rejection of the Sabbath principle and God no longer wills any kind of day of rest for people and worship is to go way beyond what Paul was saying.

Resurrection day

This is especially true since God does put the spotlight on a particular day in the New Testament. As we have already seen, the New Testament repeatedly underlines that the resurrection took place on the first day of the week and Christ continues to meet with his disciples on that day (John 20:19,24,26) and the Spirit was given on that day.

Still a one in seven pattern of gathering and worship

There was still a one in seven pattern of gathering and worship going on. By these acts which speak so eloquently of his grace, God marks out one day in seven as special—and that looks very like the Sabbath continued in principle, doesn't it?

4 Jesus and the Sabbath

None of us want to be legalistic or hypocritical Pharisees. And the Pharisees were very hot on their own version of Sabbath observance. They seem to have used the day simply to parade their own self-righteousness and to criticise and condemn others. I'm sure a right avoiding of this Pharisaism provides much of the current momentum against Sunday observance. But the baby is being thrown out with the bath water.

Jesus' rebuking the Pharisees over their *misuse* and *misunderstanding* of the Sabbath is one thing—proving that Jesus abolished the Sabbath principle altogether is quite another.

In fact, the data from the Gospels seems rather to indicate that Jesus underlined the Sabbath principle. How is Sunday special? Surely, it is special because it represents the Old Testament Sabbath principle translated into New Covenant terms. In the New Covenant the law is not abrogated but written in our hearts (Jeremiah 31:33; Romans 8:3–4).[8] Why would the Sabbath idea be set aside?

Let's think about this for a moment.

---

8   It would be extreme special pleading to argue that Jeremiah excluded the Sabbath from God's law written on the heart.

Creation

First, the Sabbath principle goes back to Creation. On the secular public stage, Christians have sadly recently lost the battle concerning the redefinition of marriage. As Christians, we looked at our Bibles and said marriage is between man and woman. That is how it was at the beginning (Matthew 19:4–5), and to change it is wrong. Just so we find the day of rest, one day in seven, was written into creation (Genesis 2:1–3).[9] Surely to ignore that is equally wrong. And notice that the Creation reference in Genesis 2 is the basis for the Fourth Commandment in Exodus 20:8–11. If we feel free to ignore creation ordinances, why did we kick up such a fuss over Same Sex Marriage?

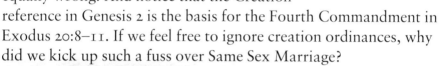

Sign of a new era

Second, the change of the day as we move into the New Testament fits the idea of the onset of the new covenant era far better than a cancelling of the Sabbath principle would.

- It is worth remembering[10] that, though the Sabbath was the seventh day of Creation, for Adam (created on the sixth day) it was the first full day of his life. Adam's first sunrise was the Sabbath. The light dawned on God's newly created world and it was the day God had blessed and made holy. The Sabbath speaks of newness.

- It is also necessary to notice that the great Old Testament redemption at the exodus apparently brought a change of calendar. By the exodus from Egypt, God effectively created

---

9   Though the word 'Sabbath' is not used here, the Hebrew verb translated 'rested' (v. 2) is the origin of the noun 'Sabbath'. Also Hebrews 4:9 links Genesis 2:1-3 with the words 'Sabbath-rest'.
10 See for example, Iain D. Campbell, *On the First Day of the Week*, DayOne publications.

Israel as a new nation—his nation. And that meant that times had changed. The beginning of the year was recalibrated reflecting the fact that a new era had dawned for Israel as they were set free from slavery. On the brink of the exodus, God says to Moses, 'This month is to be for you the first month, the first month of your year' (Exodus 12:2). God reset the months of the year.

This being so, it should not surprise us that when the great redemption, of which the exodus is only a shadow, is accomplished by Christ that this too is marked by a change of calendar. A new era has indeed dawned with the new covenant. God's holy day is not cancelled. It becomes the first day of every new week.

Lord of the Sabbath

Third, Jesus speaks of himself as Lord even of the Sabbath (Mark 2:27–28). God established the Sabbath in Genesis, so in claiming to be Lord of the Sabbath, this is another clear claim of Jesus to Deity. But notice some other things here. Some theologians (like the writers of the *ESV Study Bible* Note) insist that the Sabbath was for Israel alone. They say it can be seen simply as part of Israel's ceremonial law—now dispensed with.[11]

But in Mark's verses Jesus does not say the Sabbath was made for Israel but for man. The Sabbath being 'made' refers back to Creation. 'Man' appears to be a universal reference to mankind (Genesis 1:26–27), not just Israel. Further, Jesus uses the title 'Son of Man' in conjunction with his claim to be Lord of the Sabbath.

---

11 The texts often used to 'prove' this position by new covenant theologians are Exodus 31:12–17 and its parallel, Ezekiel 20:12–17. These verses do, indeed, say that the Sabbath was given to Israel as a sign of the covenant between God and the nation. But to infer from these texts that the Sabbath is that and that alone is a *non sequitur*. It would be like saying that because Jesus is the 'Son of Man', he is that and that only and cannot be the 'Son of God' as well. That interpretation of Exodus 31 and Ezekiel 20 reads into the text something that is not there and loads far too much theological freight upon them—especially given that the Sabbath was celebrated before Sinai in Exodus 16.

'The Son of Man is Lord even of the Sabbath' (Mark 2:28). That title is nowhere restricted to Jesus' relation to Israel but is always used in respect to the world in general. So it is with the seminal passage concerning the 'Son of Man' in Daniel 7:13–14. 'He was given authority, glory and sovereign power; all peoples, nations and men of every language worshipped him.' So, the restriction of the Sabbath principle to Israel doesn't fit.

But more, Jesus says in these verses that the Sabbath was made for man—i.e., 'for the good of man'—for rest, for renewal, for employers not to exploit their employees by making them work seven days a week as Israel had to in Egyptian slavery. It is a moral law (part of the Ten Commandments) which is a blessing to people as it commands rest for workers and legislates against their abuse. Now we have to think, with Jesus explaining that the Sabbath is a blessing to man, how does it make any sense to believe that his first move as Lord of the Sabbath will be to abolish it? It would be worse than nonsense. And what kind of Saviour would that make Jesus, as he removes God's commanded protection from ordinary working men and women? Rather he shows he is the loving Lord of the Sabbath not by abolishing it but by changing days. The Old Covenant is gone, the New has come—marked by Christ's victory being remembered every first day of the week.

The Sabbath was made for ~~Israel~~ MAN

Salvation by grace

Fourth, of course the day of rest does not just speak at the level of creation but at the level of salvation. It is a picture of grace, forgiveness and joy. It is a picture of our recognising that by our own 'working' we cannot be saved, and so we must 'rest' in Christ by believing on him. How would getting rid of the day of rest help us to be reminded to trust Christ for salvation and rest from our own workings? It wouldn't.

That's why Jesus announces salvation at the beginning of his public ministry on a Sabbath day—in the synagogue reading from Isaiah 61 of the 'Sabbath of Sabbaths'—the year of Jubilee:

> 'The Spirit of the Lord is on me,
> because he has anointed me
> to preach good news to the poor.
> He has sent me to proclaim freedom for the prisoners
> and recovery of sight for the blind,
> to release the oppressed,
> to proclaim the year of the Lord's favour'
> (Luke 4:18–19).

With the Sabbath principle standing for such good news, we can certainly understand Jesus wanting to rescue the day from the clutches of the legalistic and condemnatory Pharisees and their misuse of it. But how would it ever make sense to think that Jesus' concern was to rescind it?

Rescued not rescinded

5 The Ten Commandments

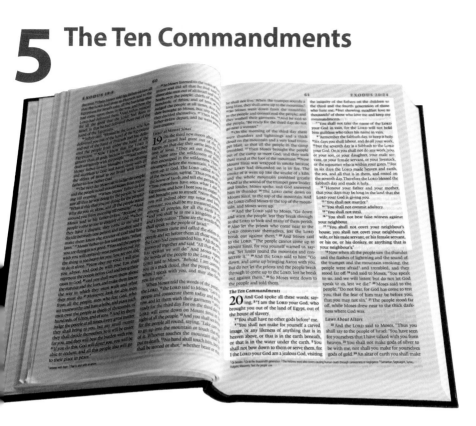

T he New Testament declares clearly that Christian love is the fulfilment of God's law (Romans 13:10), and that sin is the breaking of God's law (1 John 3:4). And it is clear from the context that what is in mind particularly when God's law is spoken of is the Ten Commandments (Romans 13:9).

So, both positively and negatively, the Decalogue furnishes the core of the Biblical ethic.

This is how Professor John Murray put it:

'When we apply the biblico-theological method to the study of Scripture it will be seen that the Ten Commandments as promulgated at Sinai were but the concrete and practical form of enunciating principles which did not then for the first time come to relevance but were relevant from the beginning. And it will also be seen that, as they did not begin to have relevance at Sinai, so they did not cease to have relevance when the Sinaitic economy had passed away. It is a biblico-theological study that demonstrates that these commandments embody principles which belong to the order which God established for man at the beginning, as also to the order of redemption.' [12]

> 'As they did not begin to have relevance at Sinai, so they did not cease to have relevance when the Sinaitic economy had passed away'

Thankfully salvation is not achieved by our own keeping of the law (Galatians 2:15–16). Salvation is by grace, through faith in our Lord Jesus Christ, who has paid for all our sins and lived a perfectly righteous life on our behalf (1 Corinthians 1:30). Jesus is our righteousness.

However, the New Testament is concerned that through love, the Christian, though never perfect in this life and always in need of grace, should seek to keep the whole law in our daily living. Once again the Ten Commandments are obviously in view as James writes:

> 'For whoever keeps the whole law and yet stumbles at just one point is guilty of breaking all of it. For he who said "Do not commit adultery," also said, "Do not murder." If you do not commit adultery but do commit murder, you have become a law-breaker' (James 2:10–11).

With James' concern that we aim to keep the whole law, how can we possibly think that it is fine for Christians to ignore the Fourth Commandment?

---

12 John Murray, *Principles of Conduct: studies in Biblical ethics* (Tyndale Press, 1971), p. 7.

From the beginning

With this in mind it is important to realise, as we have already seen, that the Sabbath command has been in place for mankind since creation.

This is clearly evidenced in the fact that the people of Israel were called to keep the Sabbath *before* the giving of the Ten Commandments at Sinai. Freshly out of Egypt and traversing the desert, Israel needed food to sustain them. The LORD provided manna in the wilderness with every dawn. We are told:

> 'Each morning everyone gathered as much as he needed, and when the sun grew hot, it melted away. On the sixth day, they gathered twice as much—two omers for each person—and the leaders of the community came and reported this to Moses. He said to them, "This is what the LORD commanded: 'Tomorrow is to be a day of rest, a holy Sabbath to the LORD. So bake what you want to bake and boil what you want to boil. Save whatever is left and keep it until morning'"' (Exodus 16:21–23).

Further, the establishment of the Sabbath from Creation is verified all through Genesis by the repeated references to 'seven days'. Noah waits seven days to send out the dove as he tests whether the waters had dried up from the earth after the Flood (Genesis 8:10,12). All of Abraham's male descendants are to be circumcised after one week of life—on the eighth day (Genesis 17:12). Jacob's working for Laban for seven years in order to marry his daughter is referred to as a 'bridal week' (Genesis 29:27), etc. The idea of the week, and therefore, by implication, the Sabbath was known to the patriarchs though probably neglected, as were many of God's other commands.

> The establishment of the Sabbath from Creation is verified all through Genesis

25

A problem?

Some Bible teachers seem confused about this evidence that the Sabbath had been commanded from the beginning because of a reference in the book of Nehemiah.

Reciting something of the history of Israel, Nehemiah writes:

> 'You came down on Mount Sinai; you spoke to them from heaven. You gave them regulations and laws that are just and right, and decrees and commands that are good. You made known to them your holy Sabbath and gave them commands, decrees and laws through your servant Moses' (Nehemiah 9:13–14).

Certainly, Israel as a nation stood out from other nations because of the Sabbath—its law for rest, even for servants (Exodus 20:10), was remarkable. But superficially this text could be read as implying that before Sinai, Israel did not have the Sabbath and therefore the command does not go back to creation and it was a law only for Israel.

However, I think that would be to take the verses the wrong way. As we have already seen, there is plenty of evidence that the command goes back to the beginning of the world. Indeed, the Ten Commandments themselves say so (Exodus 20:11). Rather, what is going on here seems best explicable in the same way that we take Exodus 6:3. In that passage God says to Moses that he is the God of Abraham, Isaac and Jacob, 'but by my name the LORD I did not make myself known to them.' However, right from the start of Abraham's experience of God, for example, we find that 'he built an altar to the LORD and called on the name of the LORD' (Genesis 12:8). There seems to be a contradiction. But there isn't. What is actually going on here is that although Abraham had known the name of the LORD, he had never experienced the totality of what that name meant. But, in the time of Moses and the exodus, that would now be experienced as God revealed his great covenant name in its full force, through the 10 great plagues and the saving of Israel through the Red Sea. 'Then you will know that I am the LORD your God' (Exodus 6:7).

Similarly, it was not that there was no Sabbath commandment before Sinai. We have already seen that there was. It was rather that Israel experienced what that meant in its fullness as God came down on Sinai and met with them. That is what Nehemiah is getting at.

The Decalogue

We should not try to set aside or divide the Ten Commandments. They were always seen as different from the other laws given to Israel.

This is indicated by the fact that they were spoken directly by God himself, at Sinai, to the people (Exodus 20:1,19). Other laws came via Moses as intermediary. Again,

> We should not try to set aside or divide the Ten Commandments

it is these ten laws alone which were inscribed 'by the finger of God' on the tablets of stone (Exodus 31:18; Deuteronomy 9:10). Furthermore, it was these tablets on which were written the Ten Commandments, which were kept within the ark of the covenant (Exodus 25:20–22; Hebrews 9:4). They are foundational and, as the citation of John Murray explained, they are all applicable as the basic ethic of the people of God in all the different phases of salvation history.

27

6 Sunday and the gospel

Sunday becomes the great day for the Christian to hear the gospel. This is because it was on Sunday, the first day of the week, that our salvation was seen to be unveiled and totally secured as the Lord Jesus rose from the grave.

The 45th question and answer of the Heidelberg Catechism summarises the connection between the gospel and the first Easter Sunday very well.

- **Question 45.** *What benefit do we receive from the resurrection of Christ?*

- **Answer:** *First*, by his resurrection he has overcome death, that he might make us partakers of the righteousness which by his death he obtained for us. *Secondly*, we also are now by his power raised up to new life. *Thirdly*, the resurrection of Christ is to us a sure pledge of our blessed resurrection.

Justification, sanctification and resurrection are here. This is all good news for sinners.

A day of good news

This is history

The first thing to say about the gospel is that it is the truth. It is not simply a theory or a combination of 'cleverly invented stories' (2 Peter 1:16). Christ actually did live on earth, die for our sins and was raised for our justification in history. This did not take place in some imaginary parallel universe but in our world—the real world—whose history is continuous down to today.

The resurrection of Christ took place on the first day of the week. So when we as churches gather on the first day of the week it is a witness to the historical facts of the gospel. If we adopt an 'any day will do—they are all the same' attitude, we are giving the impression of something different. Any day would indeed do if the gospel were just philosophy or a mystical set of ideas. But it is not. It is real. And the crowning victory of what happened—namely when sin and death were shown to be defeated as Christ rose from the grave—took place on a Sunday. Gathering to worship on a Sunday is a weekly anniversary that signifies the gospel is reality. The resurrection took place on a Sunday, and that is why, down the centuries, Christians have always met on a Sunday. The gospel is true with all its promises of forgiveness and new life in Christ.

Listen to the Word

It is fitting, therefore, that the central activity of Sunday should be to listen to the Word of God preached. It was on that first Easter Sunday that the risen Lord Jesus came to his disciples and his first word to them was, 'Peace be with you!' (John 20:19,26). The great word of peace with God is music to the ears of sinners. We need to continually hear it, for it not only brings salvation but assurance of salvation. It keeps us believing. It keeps us persevering in the faith.

Martin Luther uses Sabbath vocabulary to give both an encouragement and a warning concerning the need to regularly sit under the preaching of the gospel and meditate on God's Word:

'We teach continually, that the knowledge of Christ, and of faith, is no work of man, but simply the gift of God, who as he createth faith, so doth he keep us in it. And even as he first giveth faith unto us through the word, so afterwards he exerciseth, increaseth, strengtheneth and maketh perfect the same in us by the word.

'Therefore the greatest service that a man can do unto God, and the very Sabbath of Sabbaths, is to exercise himself in true godliness, diligently to hear and to read the word. Contrariwise, there is nothing more dangerous than to be weary of the word. He therefore that is so cold, that he thinketh himself to know enough, and beginneth by little and little to loathe the word, that man hath lost Christ and the gospel, and that which he thinketh himself to know, he attaineth only by bare speculation.'[13]

Not there yet

Our salvation is secure. Christ has won it for us by his cross. He has guaranteed it by his resurrection.

But it is not yet consummated. We are not yet in heaven. We need to keep our faith strong. Heaven is the continual Sabbath (Revelation). But we are not there yet. In the words of Hebrews 4:9, 'There remains, then, a Sabbath-rest for the people of God.' So because we have not yet arrived, Sunday is meant to operate as a foretaste and encouragement. It is meant to be special in rest, worship, peace and joy.

> Sunday is meant to operate as a foretaste and encouragement

---

13 Martin Luther, *Commentary on Galatians* (comment on Galatians 1:11–12).

7 How to spend Sundays

As we have noted, the change from Old Testament to New Testament brings a change of day with regard to the Fourth Commandment—from Saturday to Sunday.

That should bring with it something of a change of ethos for God's day. Whereas in the Old Testament the people of God could be said to be 'under law', with the coming of Christ salvation has been won, once for all, and we are now 'under grace' (Galatians 3:23–29). We are children of God through faith in our Lord Jesus Christ. The new day of rest is a day of salvation and victory. It is the day we remember that Christ has defeated sin, death, hell and Satan. Therefore, it ought to have much more of the air of celebration and exultation about it.

The Pharisees gave the Sabbath a grim and rather frowning face. As Christians, saved by grace, we need to regard the day much more positively. In our own home, we felt it was incumbent upon us to try to make Sunday the best day of the week—a day not so much of restrictions, but a day we could enjoy together to the glory of God.

How can we do that? Here are four things to think about.

- *We are to gather with the people of God and hear his Word.*
  We have already noted this, but we can see the Lord Jesus setting us the example in this. Given his 'Old Testament environment' this is what he did on the Sabbath (Mark 1:21; Mark 3:1–2, etc.). Now we have moved into New Testament times, the same applies to us. The Scriptures are to be read and preached and the Lord's Supper, reminding us of the gospel, is to be enjoyed, for our encouragement (1 Timothy 4:13; 1 Corinthians 11:33; Hebrews 10:25).

- *We are to do good works of human kindness.*

  Again, we find that the Lord Jesus is our example in this. The Sabbath always pointed forward to God's kingdom and his eternal rest which still remains for us (Hebrews 4:9). That is why the Lord Jesus performed so many of his miraculous cures on the Sabbath (John 5:9; Mark 3:4; Luke 13:10-13). He didn't do it simply to provoke the Pharisees but because it was appropriate to the joy of the world to come. Just so, on the first day of the week, the day of resurrection, we are to do good to our fellow men and women with works of kindness.

- *We are to rest from our daily employment and trust God.*

  There is always a pressure to try to earn more money. But we are not to let anxiety concerning our bank balance drive us to neglect the Lord's Day rest. The Lord Jesus defended his disciples against the hyper-critical Pharisees when they were hungry and picking ears of corn to eat as they walked through the fields on the Sabbath (Matthew 12:1–14). This wasn't pursuing business for gain; it was simply meeting a human need. The day of rest is given for our well-being.

- *We are to make it a day of family joy.*

  The idea of ceasing from our work is bound up with the idea of enjoying God's provision together as a family. It is the day when, in particular, you can sit down together, around the family meal table to enjoy the 'fruit of your labour' (Psalm 128:2). The day of rest is the time that families can spend meaningful time together.

With God and his worship at the centre of our day, these things can be worked out and worked together for our huge enjoyment and benefit.

10 out of 10

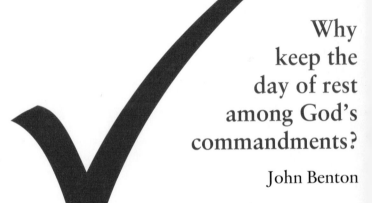

Why
keep the
day of rest
among God's
commandments?

John Benton

Dr John Benton is Director of Pastoral Support
with the Pastors' Academy
at London Seminary

Day One Publications
Ryelands Road Leominster HR6 8NZ
sales@dayone.co.uk | www.dayone.co.uk
☎ +44 (0) 1568 613 740
☎ North America Toll Free: 888 329 6630

DayOne

ISBN 978-1-84625-726-1

9 781846 257261